THE
BOARD OF DEPUTIES
OF
BRITISH JEWS
1760–1985

A Brief Survey

Aubrey Newman

VALLENTINE, MITCHELL

First published 1987 in Great Britain by
VALLENTINE, MITCHELL AND COMPANY LIMITED
Gainsborough House, 11 Gainsborough Road,
London E11 1RS, England

and in the United States of America by
VALLENTINE, MITCHELL AND COMPANY LIMITED
c/o Biblio Distribution Centre,
81 Adams Drive, P.O.Box 327, Totowa, N.J. 07511

Copyright © 1987 Aubrey Newman

British Library Cataloguing in Publication Data

Newman, Aubrey
 The Board of Deputies of British Jews,
 1760–1985 : a brief survey.
 1. Board of Deputies of British Jews —
 History
 I. Title
 941'.004924   DS135.E5

ISBN 0-85303-222-X

Library of Congress Cataloging-in-Publication Data

Newman, Aubrey.
 The Board of Deputies of British Jews, 1760–1985.

  1. Board of Deputies of British Jews. 2. Jews—
Great Britain—Societies, etc. 3. Great Britain—
Ethnic relations. I. Title.
DS135.E5N48   1987   941'.004924   87-10398
ISBN 0-85303-222-X

All rights reserved. No part of this publication may be reproduced, stored in a retrieval system, or transmitted in any form, or by any means, electronic, mechanical, photocopying, recording, or otherwise, without the prior permission of Vallentine, Mitchell and Company Limited.

*Printed and bound in Great Britain by
Robert Hartnoll [1985] Ltd., Bodmin, Cornwall*

CONTENTS

Introduction	v
Preface	vii
Early Years	1
Moses Montefiore	7
The New Community	18
The Modern Community	32
The Last Half Century	53

Dr. Lionel Kopelowitz, J.P.

INTRODUCTION
By Dr. Lionel Kopelowitz, JP
President of the Board of Deputies of British Jews

The Board of Deputies of British Jews has a long and distinguished history. Its origins date back to the accession of King George III in 1760 and from then onwards it has represented the proud Jewish community of the United Kingdom, adapting its structure and its organisation to meet the changing needs of the British Jewish community, and the variety of issues with which it has to contend.

Throughout the Nineteenth Century the activities of the Board centred on two main issues – in the first place the fight to obtain for Jews in Great Britain equality of rights at every level, and in the second to establish the tradition that the Board would intervene on behalf of all those Jewish communities beyond our shores who are unable to speak for themselves.

The problems of the Nineteenth Century are well behind us, but equally difficult problems face the Jewish community as we enter the closing years of the Twentieth Century.

We have been fortunate that Dr. Aubrey Newman, a historian of distinction, has been able to trace the history of the Board in a most engaging manner. As I read this book, I was able to look back at our past two hundred and twenty-five years with pleasure and with pride. Indeed a study of history and of the achievements of the past is an excellent guide in plotting and charting the future.

I commend this book to all those who have a keen interest in the roots of our community, and I know that they will derive much strength from its contents.

PREFACE

This is not a history of the Board, but rather a study of some aspects of it written for a particular occasion. It would not have been possible to have written the full history which the institution deserves, and the way is still open for that larger work. In the meantime I express my appreciation for the opportunity to view the Board against the background of the community as a whole, and to express what is after all an entirely personal view.

Not all historians of British Jewry will agree with the comments I have made, but I hope that they would agree that the conclusions are not out of line with the ways in which the evidence has presented itself and the community has developed. Within the time which was available much of the basic work which should have been done could not have been undertaken. Instead I have drawn upon a wide variety of other historians' work. Israel Cohen and Adolph Brotman wrote two earlier outlines of the history of the Board and I am grateful to have been shown their manuscripts.

There are many who will recognise echoes of their own words: Geoffrey Alderman, Stuart Cohen, Judge Israel Finestein, Colin Holmes, Bernard Homa, Barry Kosmin, Gisella Lebzelter, Schneier Levenberg, David Rosenberg and Gideon Shimoni. There are many others on whom I have drawn to a greater and lesser degree; to all of them I express my appreciation. If they are not named specifically it is because the bibliography of a community is difficult to compile, certainly in so short a study as this.

I must conclude, of course, by acknowledging the freedom given to me to write the study. The comments and conclusions are entirely mine, and in no way is it to be taken as reflecting the views of anyone other than myself.

Aubrey Newman

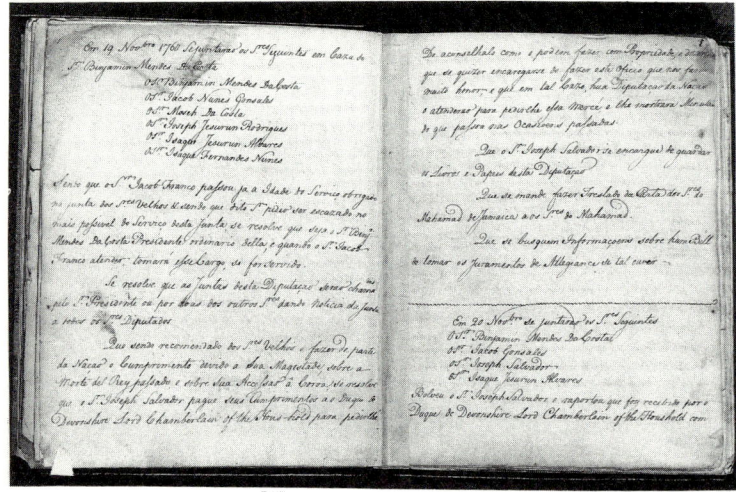

First minutes of the Board (in Portuguese), 10th November 1760

MINUTES   17 Nov 85 (Contd)

between East and West, and that those who cherish freedom will be the beneficiaries of such change.

"We think, at this moment, of our brethren in the Soviet Union, we think of Anatoli Scharansky, and the Prisoners of Conscience, and we shall, later this morning, hold a special meeting to give expression to our concerns and hopes.

"Nearer home, we were satisfied to learn that the Greater London Council did not agree to make a grant of about £27,000 to a PLO front organisation which had been described by Sir Ashley Bramall, a former Chairman of ILEA, as "bogus".   This was only achieved because certain members of the majority group broke party discipline and refused to support this recommendation, and we congratulate them on their courage and perception.   They truly represent the citizens of London.

"The Board's response to the Report of the Farm Animal Welfare Council has now been completed.   In accordance with our usual practice, we sought guidance from our Ecclesiastical Authorities on this matter, and also carried

Minutes (extract), 17th November 1985

EARLY YEARS

The history of the Board of Deputies illustrates clearly various facets of the history of the wider British Jewish community.

Its institutions reflect the various strains and tensions within the wider body, but their development is very often also a reflection of the individual personalities who control them. The various Presidents of the Board, for example, have put their own impress on the ways in which the Board reacted, or failed to react, to various points of crisis within the community.

The Board reflects also however one of the peculiar features of the British Jewish community, the way in which it came into existence. Many of the communities on the continent of Europe came into being as the result of a deliberate act of will on behalf of the ruler. He issued an invitation for the creation of the community, but on terms laid down by him, and he would usually create some apparatus by which regular contact was established between him and them. The 'Kehilla' would then exist as a formal body, responsible for such relations, responsible for taxation, internal policing and regulation, and for the general supervision of the community.

No such institution was created for the original British Jewish community. Indeed there was no formal 'instrument' by which Jews were ever invited to return to the country. If any such instrument had ever existed it was long since destroyed, and the original community in London quietly developed and found a place in the life of the capital.

No specific system of taxation was ever created and no restrictions on their place of abode were ever imposed on them. They were subject to the same laws as any other inhabitants in the country, and when their children were born in the country they acquired the same rights of citizenship as any other native-born British subjects.

The restrictions by which they were bound were the same as

many of their fellow citizens also experienced. Only members of the Church of England were eligible for a wide variety of offices in the State; the Test Acts of 1673 laid down as an essential pre-requisite of holding of office the possession of a sacrament certificate, proving that its holder had presented himself at a regular service of Communion and had thereby conformed to the dominant Church.

No Roman Catholic or strict Protestant Dissenter could thereafter hope to hold such office, nor could any Jew be regarded as eligible. But in all other respects Jews were as full citizens as any other groups in the Kingdom.

The first organised Jewish communities in London appeared during the middle of the seventeenth century and were composed of Sephardi Jews, Spanish and Portuguese, either escaping by devious means from the Spanish Peninsula or coming from the already established communities of Amsterdam. It might well be that so long as there was only one community in London there was no real need for any overall supervision, but certainly the arrival of a number of refugees from Central and Eastern Europe, the Ashkenazi Jews, led to the establishment of a new community, and speedily enough to several new bodies.

None of these congregations would have much to do with each other, and this early community seems to have been more conspicuous for its fissipariness than for its communal cohesion. But there were very few occasions for any of them to come into formal contact with the governing elements of the State.

There were a number of such contacts during the first sixty years of the eighteenth century. In 1744 for instance, when the Jews of Prague were expelled from that city by the Empress Maria Theresa, appeals were made to all the Jewish communities of Europe and the leaders of the (Ashkenazi) Great Synagogue had an audience with the King, George II, asking him to intercede; the King 'with tears in his eyes' promised to do what he could. There was certainly however no attempt made to secure joint action.

EARLY YEARS

At various times during these years the Sephardi congregation felt itself potentially affected by various actions of the British government. A bill had been introduced into the Irish House of Commons to make it possible to secure naturalisation in Ireland without the necessity of producing a 'sacrament' certificate; the Sephardi congregation agreed to set up a Committee of Diligence, 'senhores deputados', 'to make use of any opportunity that there may be for the benefit of the nation'. The extent of the powers and the scope of this committee remain vague, and it is not clear even how many times it met. There was certainly a considerable degree of opposition by some of the members of the congregation to any idea that the Congregation could ever claim to speak or act on behalf of the community as a whole in relation to the King and his ministers.

In 1753 for instance, the Government was asked by some of the congregation to introduce a bill into Parliament which would have allowed foreign-born Jews to acquire British nationality (by way of an expensive private act of parliament) without first having to 'conform' to the Established Church. The result was a widespread furore, which so worried the Ministers that this 'Jew Bill' was hastily repealed the following year.

One of the members of the Sephardi community was Samson Gideon, a prominent financier who felt no need for the bill since he himself was British by birth, and he wrote angrily to the community:

> Gentlemen,
> Your assuming a power of representing me in point of political or Civil Interest, as I understand you have done ... is certainly as little consistent with prudence, as with the Law of Nature, or of the Land ... Take notice, that I for my Self do in the most solemn manner disavow all power you may at any time have assumed, in civil or secular Affairs, and more especially that, which you, without any

Colour, have taken upon Your Selves to represent the Jews in general, and to request things in their names, or undertake for them, in any manner whatever.

Few would have taken such drastic action as did Gideon, but certainly there was as yet no suggestion of any possibility of collective action. Perhaps the only thing on which the members of this congregation would agree came up in October 1760, on the death of George II and the accession of George III. The committee, of seven, three of whom were to be a quorum, and to give this body the responsibility of drawing up a loyal address to the new sovereign and of dealing thereafter 'with the most urgent matters which present themselves in connection with our nation'. A loyal address was duly presented, but almost immediately difficulties arose; the German congregations – now three in number – came and complained that no account had been taken of them.

Even when it was agreed that a joint address should be made to the King's mother, the Ashkenazi congregations still requested 'that each nation should communicate to the other what they were doing in public affairs'. To the response by the Sephardi Deputies that there was no organised committee to represent the German Jews, the latter set up such a body. The Minute Book of the Great Synagogue formally records a letter from the head of the Sephardim, Joseph Salvador:

> I am order'd by the Committee of our Elders which is appointed to Look after our publick affairs that in consequence of your desire we have made an Entry of the names of the Gentlemen your Synagogue have appointed as Committee for the same purposes. And ... we have made the following Entry ... Resolved that whenever any publick affair should offer that may Intrest the Two Nations we will on our parts Communicate to the Committee of the Dutch Jews Synagogues what we may think proper should be Done. And that we desire the said

EARLY YEARS

Gentlemen may do the same and make a Minute thereof.

It has been this minute, of 14th December 1760, which has by custom been taken as indicating the establishment of the London Committee of Deputies. The name itself indicates the parallels which must always be made between the London Jewish community and its non-Jewish hosts. For in 1732, when the various non-conformist bodies in and around the capital had wanted to make joint representations to the principal ministers of the day, they had formed themselves together into the London Board of Dissenting Deputies. The parallel is clear.

What is perhaps less clear is the extent to which this new departure among the Jewish communities had any permanence. Thereafter the meetings of this new committee were very infrequent: many of the few meetings which are recorded are quite clearly of the Sephardi Deputies alone; if at times there is mention that the 'Dutch' Jews be informed of what has been decided it is clear that such meetings are unusual.

The early moves towards the removal of disabilities on British Jews were also responsible for the earliest formulation of a Constitution for the Board. In 1817 an attempt had been made to improve upon the informality of the earlier arrangements; after a five-year period during which no meeting had been held the Deputies met and agreed that 'independent of the established right of the President to call a meeting of the United Deputies of the four City Congregations at any time he should think proper' any five members could requisition one themselves.

This does not seem to have made much difference, for it was some eleven years before the group met again to transact business of significance, and then only as a result of an initiative taken by a non-member, anxious to secure relief from Parliament from the various civil disabilities under which Jews suffered.

So long as the other communities which were not part of the Established Church still suffered these same disabilities there had been little or no feelings of annoyance from the Jewish community. But when these communities were given relief from these disabilities some of the leading Jews were anxious to secure the same relief.

It was in 1828 that the Deputies met – for the first time for eight years – to draw up a petition to the House of Lords on the subject of relief of Jewish disabilities. There was no reaction to this, and it was not until the next year that the Deputies once again came together to discuss a letter from Isaac Lyon Goldsmid reporting the steps he had taken on his own initiative towards Jewish relief.

It was clear however that he had created a great deal of animosity between himself and the Board, because he had to give assurances that he would not take any public steps or make any decisions without consultation with the Deputies. On the initiative now of the Rothschilds, who had already been in touch with leading members of the Government, it was agreed to present a further petition to the House of Lords.

The Government declined to give any support, and so the matter was dropped. In practice the four parent synagogues were unwilling to incur expense on a topic in which it was clear they had little direct interest, and the only move towards the future was an agreement that a small committee should be set up to assist the President, and that there should be on it a representative from each congregation.

MOSES MONTEFIORE

Moses Montefiore became President of the Committee in 1835, and for the next forty years was the dominating influence on it. At various times there were other Presidents – usually standing in during his absences overseas – but until he finally retired from office in 1874 he virtually personified the institution.

Certainly these were the years in which much of its character was established, largely through the impress of his own personality and for better or for worse it was virtually his creation. But the seeds of future weaknesses were also sown during this period, and some of the discords which appeared later in its history can be seen already in these years.

It can well be argued that it was only during his presidency that the Board even came into existence. What had previously been an occasional gathering together of representatives of some (not all) of the main London synagogues as and when it was felt to be expedient now became a consciously formulated body. A gathering in 1835 of these representatives agreed on a number of resolutions:

> This meeting is convinced it would be of essential advantage to the interests of the Jews in Britain, that in all matters touching their political welfare they should be represented by one body, and inasmuch as the general body of Deputies have long been recognised as their representatives it is highly desirable for the general good that all the British Jews should so acknowledge them, having a sufficient number of Members from each congregation to ensure the accordance of their proceedings with the general wishes of the Jews.

These resolutions also dealt with the allocation of expenses among the various member congregations, and invited the

THE BOARD OF DEPUTIES OF BRITISH JEWS

Sir Moses Montefiore, Bart., 1784–1885

participation in this body of any other 'Congregation of Jews in the United Kingdom'. It is clear that there were many already who would not have accepted the premise that the old committee of Deputies had been so recognised as widely 'representative', and the reality behind this body was the move to secure relief from political disabilities, similar to that secured by the Roman Catholic and Protestant dissenting congregations.

In practice however the agitation for political emancipation rapidly acquired a momentum of its own in which the Board as an institution had little or no part, while it also soon became clear that there were two distinct threads to it. One group desired as much 'emancipation' as could be secured without any sacrifice of the separateness and distinctiveness of British Jewry, while the other group was prepared to achieve full political and social integration even if that implied an erosion of some parts of Jewish separateness.

It was clear too that there were many within the community who were not content merely to rank themselves behind the President and the Board, who maintained very strongly that the Board did not possess a monopoly of political action within the wider community. Indeed, even from the beginning, there were many who called into question the extent of the representative nature of the Board and the limitations of its claim to speak on behalf of provincial Jewry.

So early indeed were the lines established of conflicts which were to reappear at various stages during the next hundred and fifty years. From the outset open opposition was expressed about the clause of the original constitution laying down that the Board was to be the only official channel of communication with the British government in political matters affecting British Jews. It was alleged that the Board was too unwieldy, that it acted far too slowly, and that it could not be said to be representative of all the communities within the country as a whole.

That it was largely a London organisation was in practice very true, but it must be said that that was as much the result of

THE BOARD OF DEPUTIES OF BRITISH JEWS

Sir David Salomons, Bart.,
Lord Mayor of London, 1855

various provincial communities having declined membership as that of a desire by the London 'Grandees' to exclude them. Within London the small congregations of St Alban's Place and Maiden Lane affiliated, but in the provinces Edinburgh had declined, Birmingham took no decision, Liverpool wanted time to consider, Gloucester acknowledged the invitation, Yarmouth felt that it was in no position to agree, Chatham refused and Sunderland agreed to make a nomination. Even this soon lapsed on grounds of poverty, so that the Board's initial attempt to extend membership was not exactly successful.

Nonetheless strong resentment was expressed, and one of the protagonists of this discontent was specifically invited to discuss the issue with the Board. It was finally agreed that no individuals would be precluded from taking such private actions as they felt desirable, but the issue remained very lively. Given the circumstances in which the original group had been brought together in 1760 it was to be even more annoying in 1840 when one individual synagogue, at the instigation of one of these dissidents, presented its own loyal address on the Queen's marriage instead of associating itself with the Board as a whole.

One of the earliest official recognitions of the Board, and one which certainly gave it widespread authority, came through two acts of Parliament, the Marriage and Registration Acts. Under these, the laws of England recognised the rights of Jewish congregations to conduct lawful marriages and to register them, provided that they had appointed a duly recognised and registered 'marriage secretary'.

The responsibility for recommending such a suitable person lay with the 'London Committee of Deputies of the British Jews'. The President was given as a result a considerable degree of authority over all the congregations of Jews in Great Britain.

It became important also to ensure not merely that the various synagogues in the country be properly registered but that they conformed strictly to the law of the land. The secular and religious laws could on occasion come into conflict; religious law permitted the marriage of uncle and niece but secular English law did not.

Again, there were perpetual conflicts over the desire of some religious authorities to issue religious divorces which could not be recognised by civil authorities and which might in consequence lead to problems over subsequent remarriage. There were to be occasions certainly when Montefiore would have liked to see some virtual enclave in which Jews could live out their lives within the framework of religious laws, while his opponents inside and outside the Board were far more anxious to see British Jewry fully integrated within the wider community.

The necessity of securing recognition from the Board gave the Board and its Officers a considerable degree of power over the various congregations in the country. The responsibility was exercised however in conjunction with the recognised religious authorities of the country – the Chief Rabbi for the Ashkenazi communities, the Haham for the Sephardim.

But this too in its turn could lead to further complications, for it could be used to ensure that all communities toed the line as conceived by Montefiore. The issue came to the fore over the emergence of the (Reform) West London Congregation of British Jews. This had developed as a breakaway from the existing London congregations and was opposed by them.

The antagonism developed so far as to lead them to be excommunicated. Even though some of his own family were closely involved with the new congregation, Montefiore was bitterly opposed to it, and it was largely his influence which prevented any degree of recognition of it by the Board. It was refused recognition for marriage purposes, while no compromise could allow it to become a member of the Board.

He refused to accede even to the suggested compromise that it be regarded as 'a synagogue of persons professing the Jewish religion'. The extent to which his animosity was carried became clear in 1853 when the police were called to a meeting of the Board. Four members of the Reform Congregation had been elected as Deputies from various provincial congregations; Montefiore refused to recognise the validity of their elections, and insisted that they be excluded.

What was at stake was a basic conflict of classes and of attitudes. Montefiore conceived the community as subject still to a conventional paternalism, vested in himself; he certainly did not consider that the new body whose emergence he had facilitated could be meant to fetter his own personal authority. Against him were the newly emerging Jewish middle classes who felt that the Board should represent more closely all the elements of the community, both in London and in the wider community.

Behind all this activity at the 'top' of the policy-making end of the Board was a wide range of other activities, increasingly involving the provincial communities. The appointment of salaried officers of the Board – a secretary in 1837 (Sampson Samuel), an assistant in 1860 (Lewis Emanuel) – made possible such an extension, so that the Board could begin in 1849 to make itself responsible for the collection of a wide range of statistical information.

It was decided that the Board should collect from each congregation, whether it was represented on the Board or not, details of births, marriages, deaths, and numbers of seat holders, these being printed in Annual Reports produced by the Board. Attempts were made also to estimate the total number of the Jewish population.

In 1881 for instance the suggestion was made that the population had reached 62,656, but the Board was prepared to admit that the true figure was probably much smaller, and that the statistical formula on which the figures had been based was probably misleading.

Another interest of the Board shown from the correspondence and minute books of these years was education. Between 1850 and 1872 there was a stream of national agitation over the use of State grants for schools and the Board did its best to secure for the various Jewish schools a share of these grants. The Protestant Nonconformist and Roman Catholic schools could receive them, and the Board claimed that the Jewish schools too ought to be recipients.

The case was fought over the Manchester Jewish Free School, but the victory applied to the others as well. The Board was continuously involved too in attempts to ensure that various Examining Boards should not discriminate against observant Jews by holding examinations on Sabbaths and Festivals.

A third 'domestic' matter related to various Factory Acts, whereby Sunday labour had been coming under restrictions; increasingly the Board found itself involved in securing exemption for Jewish businesses which had been closed on a Saturday and sought permission to open on a Sunday but at the same time in pointing out the need to observe these same acts in full in order to secure their full benefits.

Inevitably therefore the Board found itself in a quandary as to whether it should shut its eyes to known breaches of these Factory Acts, or whether it should, in order to retain its opportunities of intervention on behalf of the community, report them to the factory inspectorate.

The most obvious and most spectacular work of the Board in these years was clearly in the field of foreign affairs. Inevitably, as in the past, Jewish communities under peril from persecution or even under tremendous financial strain appealed to their brethren elsewhere to help them and now it was the Board which tried to take action on behalf of British Jewry.

The most obvious interventions were made by the President of the Board on its behalf. Sir Moses travelled to the Middle East on the occasion of the Damascus Blood Libel, to Russia and Roumania, to Italy on the Mortara case, to Morocco – these represent a small fraction of the numerous calls on the Board. But they highlighted not merely his own prestige and status within the Jewish and non-Jewish communities; they emphasised the significance of the Board as well.

So that even if in many ways Sir Moses Montefiore represented a comparatively stultifying influence on the Board he did much also to raise its general status. It remains nonetheless a significant fact that at the time of his final retirement from the Presidency of the Board in 1874, British Jewry was bitterly divided, and that as a result of his own actions. The refusal to allow the seating of members of the Reform community on the Board had meant the exclusion of many of the most important and most energetic of the British Jewish figures from communal life.

To try and meet that need, the Anglo-Jewish Association had been set up; the treaty between the AJA and the Board in 1878, four years after Sir Moses' retirement, was a recognition that the breach had to be healed in some manner or other.

By the late nineteenth century the Board had undergone a number of constitutional changes and developments. Some of these reflected the changing nature of the Jewish population both in London and the provinces, and partly the growth of new problems.

During the earlier years much of the section in the Annual Reports of the Board headed 'Home Affairs' dealt with ceremonial public matters – royal celebrations or royal obituaries for example – but as the century went on the character of the Board's activities changed. The very composition of the Board itself changed, and many more Deputies appeared representing the provincial and smaller communities.

The effectiveness of a specific community's representation depended on its Deputy; in many cases the question was whether a synagogue could afford the luxury of a Deputy at all. Between 1851 and 1883 the method of representation was that the running costs of the organisation were apportioned to each congregation according to the number of its Deputies. This meant that the amount due per Deputy varied with the Board's expenses and the number of Deputies.

For example, in 1853 there were 58 Deputies and the levy was £1. 19. 3d for the half year for each Deputy. By 1859 the number of Deputies had fallen to 25 and the half-yearly levy had risen to £6. 16. 4d. This system obviously penalised the small and poorer communities which might find themselves with a comparatively large bill to pay at the end of each half year. Thus in 1859 the Bath Synagogue informed the Board that it was unable to meet its arrears of £12. 11. 11d. In 1871, Article 6 of the Constitution stated that 'all congregations of Jews in the United Kingdom might elect one deputy and if they had more than 200 male members they could elect a second deputy'. However there was still nothing to alleviate the plight of the small communities until finally on 23rd February 1883 a conference to revise the Constitution was convened.

As a result of this, Clause 31 of the new Constitution instituted a Capitation Allowance for smaller communities. Part of this clause stated:

> That all the expenses of the Board shall be assessed upon and paid by the congregations represented at the Board in the following manner.
>
> Each provincial congregation, the male renters of seats on the 1st day of Iyar in any year that shall not exceed altogether one hundred in number but shall comprise ten male renters of one year's standing or upwards being *bona fide* residents in the town in which the synagogue or congregation is situate shall contribute towards the expenses of the Board for the next ensuing year a sum of 2/- for each and every male renter of a seat in the congregation on the aforesaid 1st day of Iyar; the residue of such expenses for the same year shall be contributed by all other representative congregations proportionately.

Thereafter the smaller congregations could be represented on the Board and know at the beginning of the year exactly how much they would have to contribute. When the constitution was again revised in 1881 it was decided to fix the maximum levy for each Deputy at £9 per annum. Many of these Deputies from the provincial congregations were in effect 'carpet-baggers', individuals who had little or no direct link with the congregations for which they sat at the Board.

Even when the Board had a larger number of provincial congregations represented on it than from London, the proportion of London-based Deputies remained high. It was only gradually that this proportion changed. In 1853 there were 58 Deputies of whom 26 represented six London synagogues and 32 represented 28 provincial congregations; six of this latter group had London addresses.

In 1883 there were 27 Deputies for 14 London and 18 for 18 provincial congregations; five of this latter group lived in London. In 1898 30 Deputies were elected by 17 London synagogues, 24 by provincial, and one by a colonial synagogue. This last was a Londoner, and five of the provincial Deputies had London addresses.

At the same time there was also a growing desire by many of the communities now represented on the Board to have some sort of supervision of the Board's actions. Thus there was a constitutional revision in 1850 which required the Board, except in cases of emergency, to report a wide range of intended actions to constituent congregations before action was taken, thus establishing some, albeit limited, degree of control.

This was soon to be followed by the admission of the press – i.e. the *Jewish Chronicle* – to meetings of the Board. The publication of Annual Reports was a further part of this general process. But the whole issue of the relative status of the Board with regard to the community at large was brought under close examination as a result of the greatly increased population which now arose.

THE NEW COMMUNITY

The most important consequence of the immigrations from Eastern Europe during the last quarter of the nineteenth century was the creation of what was virtually a new community. The old institutions remained and old leadership remained, at least for the moment; some of the old tensions remained too, but all were subtly changed as a result of the new numbers and the new communities which appeared.

Obviously the Board itself could not remain immune from these developments. The very introduction of large numbers of foreign-born Jews created and revealed considerable differences of wealth, social status, and indeed outlook between those who had just landed and those who had 'arrived'. With the best will in the world there were going to be considerable problems of adaptation, and the newer arrivals were going to face considerable problems with regard to their legal and social position. They were not accustomed to regarding civil authority as being not unfriendly, and the newer arrivals faced some problems in reconciling their religious practices with the law of the land. Problems such as 'illegal' marriages or unrecognised divorces were looked at differently from the perspectives of the acculturated Jew and the new immigrant. Equally, there were problems arising out of the new areas of Jewish settlement. Although the East End was not a 'new' area there grew up in it a large number of 'new' congregations, and these too in their turn eventually wished for representation at the Board; even if some of their Deputies were in practice 'West Enders' the gradual absorption of the new arrivals led to their demanding direct representation.

Many too felt that the old concept of representation through synagogal membership was no longer relevant, and pressure grew for representation through such secular bodies as the Friendly Societies. Outside London these years saw a growth

THE NEW COMMUNITY

in the provincial communities, in terms of their number and size, and the result was a strengthening of the pressure on the Board for effective representation and participation in the Board's decision making procedures.

This became the keynote of the struggles of the early twentieth century.

There was a wide range of internal conflicts, all reiterating complaints about the secretive nature of the Board's deliberations and the problems of stirring the Board to action. The pogrom at Kishineff, pending Governmental legislation (such as the Aliens Act of 1905 or measures affecting Shechita), outbreaks of anti-semitism in various parts of the country – these were issues on which the alleged inaction or reluctance of the Board to stir itself came under open attack.

By 1911 opposition to the leadership of the Board had become vocal, and motions hostile to the leadership had been the subject of debates and votes at meetings of the Board. More significantly still, organisations had appeared which threatened to rival the Board as the effective representative body of British Jewry.

Just as in an earlier generation the Anglo-Jewish Association had been founded in part to attract those excluded from the Board, so now the B'nai B'rith developed a Lodge which expressed the dissatisfaction felt by many at what they considered to be the 'oligarchy, autocracy, traditionalism, and narrow insularity' of the Board.

The resentment was also felt outside London; Manchester was prominent in its demands that the Board adapt itself to the needs of the wider community. One group there took political initiatives, setting up an independent 'agency and intelligence department' and pushing a series of demands which eventually had to be taken seriously. They called for Sunday meetings of the Board, regular reports on the Foreign Committee's activities, and a curtailment of timewasting ceremonial matters.

The issues at stake were effectively summarised by the *Jewish Chronicle*:

What the community needs is an elected body which shall be representative of the community in the broadest and completest manner practically possible. The community needs a representative body which will voice its opinions either in defence or defiance, armed with the backing of popular representation and popular support. It does not require ... a mere dunghill on which chosen cocks may crow to their sweet content.

The Board was not alone in being the recipient of these complaints; virtually every institution in British Jewry was coming under scrutiny. It was the result of the way in which the newer arrivals had begun to integrate themselves into the older institutions, and to demand for themselves the same opportunities in communal affairs which had been gained by their predecessors. The outbreak of the First World War to a limited extent defused the immediate pressures, but a number of issues began once more to raise pressure, and such issues appeared as the conscription of Russian-born Jews into either the British or Russian armies.

The crunch came however over a very different issue, one which has entered into the mythology of British Jewish history and particularly into the histories of the Board and the English Zionist Federation.

The growth of Zionism in Britain had always been accompanied by the realisation – from Herzl onwards – that it might well be necessary for the movement to 'capture' for the cause the existing institutions of the community, especially the Board. But although there were Zionists and Zionist sympathisers on various bodies, including the Board, they were in no way anywhere near being a numerically significant group.

What they were able to do however was to attempt to develop links with the grievances expressed on the Board, and they were to do that with spectacular, if short-lived, success in June 1917. The occasion was the introduction of a vote of censure on the President of the Board who had, some three weeks earlier, signed an anti-Zionist Manifesto which was published in *The Times*. The vote was carried, by 56 to 51 with six abstentions. The President of the Board resigned, and the British Government moved thereafter towards the issue of the Balfour Declaration.

On the face of it this vote implies a considerable victory for the 'Zionist Lobby' on the Board; in fact a closer examination of the details of the vote reveals a far deeper seated series of problems facing the Board and the wider community of which this vote was but a symptom. At the previous elections to the Board 143 Deputies had been elected; 45 of them represented congregations in London, 9 in the Colonies, and 89 in the Provinces. In fact many of the provincial representatives were Londoners who had sought seats elsewhere, as were the 'Colonials'; it was possible to represent a congregation at the Board without being resident within that congregation.

When complaints had been made earlier about the practice, one of the officers of the Board commented: 'if these congregations liked to sell their inheritance for a mess of pottage, that was their own affair.' The over-representation was not merely one of London as against the provinces; the mass of these 'carpet-baggers' were members from the North-West of London, so that synagogues like Brondesbury or Bayswater were very well represented, while the East End and to a lesser extent the North of London were barely represented at all.

Among the provincial Deputies the bulk of those who were 'genuinely' provincial represented the larger communities which had expanded and developed as a result of the new immigrations, and largely were in close touch with the politics and feelings of their localities. An analysis therefore of the voting patterns, linked with the previous patterns of attendance, has thrown considerable light upon the nature of the coalition which so narrowly defeated the President.

In no way can it be taken as a victory for a strong Zionist group, nor can it possibly be interpreted as a Zionist 'take-over'; the Zionist elements on the Board had in effect joined hands with a large variety of other discontented groups within the Board and the community, while the newer communities and elements had served notice that the Board had to adapt its practices and concepts to newer ideas and newer communities. The 'new generations' were flexing their muscles, and the Board would have to take account of them.

The Zionists might blithely have assumed that they had already captured the Board, but they were unable to secure the election of Zionists into such executive offices as President, Vice-President, or Treasurer. On the other hand the 'rebels' were anxious to ensure that their actions were not treated as a momentary aberration, and they engaged in a long campaign which eventually ensured a series of reforms in the Board.

Female Deputies were admitted as nominees of the Union of Jewish Women, and the seats allotted to the United Synagogue and the Federation of Synagogues were redistributed between the individual congregations and the overall synagogal organisations. The most revolutionary changes however involved the whole concept of membership of the Board. It had originally come into existence through the collective action of individual synagogues, and whenever it had thereafter expanded it had done so in terms of further synagogues being added to the existing lists. What had never been envisaged was a community where appreciable sections did not necessarily regard synagogue membership as being the basis of their communal affiliation or identification, but that was now the new nature of the British Jewish community.

As a result of the changes after 1919, Deputies could be elected on behalf of a number of secular societies and associations, including the Jewish members of the Universities of Oxford and Cambridge. These reforms however had not come as a result of Zionist interventions; indeed many of the Zionists objected strongly to the changes. Rather, they came almost as much from the 'Old Guard' who saw in them possibilities of curbing the Zionist elements.

Even the victory by which the link with the AJA through the Conjoint Foreign Committee had been dissolved, following the vote on the Board, was followed speedily by the creating of

THE NEW COMMUNITY

a new body, the Joint Foreign Committee, constituted along the same lines as the earlier body. As a result the Zionist group had to begin to think of a much longer term policy, the creation of a specific party organisation within the Board itself.

> We must form a Zionist party with Whips and endeavour to fill every vacancy with Zionists. It should definitely declare that its organisation is not intended to affect the ordinary work of the Board or to introduce any kind of party vote but to create an organisation which would secure proper representation in full force on the Board when Palestine and related questions come up for discussion. We must have a central organisation for that... There should be a provincial whip or whips and a London whip or whips and we should keep an account of the names of every member of the Board who is in sympathy and who is summoned to a special meeting.

The defeats suffered by the Zionists on the Board were, they felt, largely due to the community's oligarchic government, 'a small governing class, who have been able to usurp positions of authority chiefly owing to their wealth'. For their part the 'Old Guard' could well riposte – 'Were the Deputies, which for over 170 years had been the representative body of Anglo-Jewry, to be ruled by a policy dictated by the newly arrived in this country?'

The change in the nature of membership was reflected in the nature of the issues with which the Board now had to deal. Both in 'foreign' affairs and in domestic the Board had to assume a much more active and even perhaps raucous role. There had always been, of course, concern for the affairs of Jews abroad. But with the drastic reshaping of Europe into new strongly nationalistic states from which the Jewish minorities were almost automatically excluded there were much stronger reasons for the Board to be concerned, and the rise of the virulent anti-semitism of Hitler's Germany brought many more problems.

Domestically there were the routine matters affecting the community – the defence of Shechita, the regulation of marriages, a watchful eye on Sunday trading, and the general pattern of legislation – intermingled with defence of the community against growing threats of anti-semitism.

The issue of anti-semitism and the nature of the community's reaction to it was one which looms large in the history of the Board during the 'inter-war' years. There had been manifestations of it even before the First World War, but they had never been regarded as important, and the attitude of the Board, as of the leaders of the community, had tended to be dismissive. It had usually been regarded as an aspect of anti-alien feeling, and certainly the Board had been active in trying to damp that down.

When, for example, there had been set up before the First World War a Royal Commission on Alien Immigration the evidence given by the Board had been to try and minimise the numbers involved in the non-transient immigration, emphasising rather the contribution which had been made to the country at large. Equally, of course, the Board had been anxious to try and ensure a minimum of publicity and itself to regulate so far as was practicable issues which might cause some public antagonism, such as Sunday trading or Sunday baking. This approach, of 'acculturation' and minimal public response, was carried over into the post-war period, but seemed far less attractive in terms of contemporary Jewish and non-Jewish response.

The rise of political movements both in Britain and abroad which for the first time were avowedly rather than incidentally anti-semitic, did create problems for the Board. At first its reactions were that the Board could not enter into any active politics within the wider community, and that in any case anti-semitism was very much a minor affair. The Board had on occasion to try to ensure that anti-Bolshevism did not become anti-semitism, but the bulk of the complaints about anti-semitism with which the Board had to deal related to publishing ventures which seem to have been comparatively short-

THE NEW COMMUNITY

lived, so that the Annual Reports of the Board could comment that it was 'now rare to find anything to which exception might be taken'.

The significant change came in the 1930s, and reflected the growth of a 'populist' aspect to British Fascism, particularly in the East End, the desires of British Jewry to find some effective and practical way of giving assistance to a growing stream of refugees from Germany, and the emergence of a new generation of Jews, this time from the East End, who felt that the traditional leadership of British Jewry, be it lay or religious, had little or nothing to offer them.

The Board's basic approach to the rise of Mosley's Fascism, and to its attempt to stir up trouble through a series of public demonstrations of 'strength', had been to try and keep matters quiet, to try and avoid provoking trouble, and certainly to avoid giving the British Union of Fascists any opportunity of causing trouble.

The Board's attitude reflected also its approach, in 'foreign affairs', to the rise of Hitler's Germany. It was not, for example, until November 1934 that the Board publicly endorsed the 'Boycott German Goods' campaign which had been launched in March 1933.

When therefore anti-semitism began to make significant reappearances in Great Britain the Board was content to rely on the normal apparatus of the State. The leadership of the Board was therefore happy to remain comparatively quiescent, to prefer indirect pressure upon the Government and police, to issue propaganda designed to illustrate the Jewish contribution to Britain and civilisation, to draw attention away from so-called Jewish failings in areas which were supposed to be areas of dense Jewish population and to maintain a low profile by staying away from provocative meetings.

Many of the British Jewish population were not so content, and the result was yet another conflict within the community. There were complaints that the leadership of the Board was out of touch with the 'rank and file', and a series of conflicts developed between what soon appeared under the aegis of the

Board as the 'Co-ordinating Committee ... to unify and direct activities in defence of the Jewish communities against attacks made upon it' – (soon renamed the Defence Committee) – and a newly created Jewish People's Council set up to attack not only anti-semitism but also, directly and by name, Fascism.

The JPC claimed to represent all Jews within its movement and attacked the supineness of the Board; the Board for its part condemned the 'unauthorised activities of the so-called Jewish People's Council which ... had assumed functions which only the Board was entitled to exercise'. The split was not, of course, merely one between these two organisations. Many of the respected leaders of the Board were equally unhappy about the apparent lack of guidance from the Board, and the Vice-President, Sir Robert Waley Cohen, was amongst those who tried to urge the President to action.

The Co-ordinating Committee was one of the Board's responses, and certainly it was very effective behind the scenes. More prominent were the attempts by the community to monitor on its own account possible 'Jewish causes' of anti-semitism. Accusations of unfair trading and cut-price tactics were commonly held to refer to actions by Jews; it was often claimed that wicked Jewish landlords had been involved in unfair practices. Vigilance committees and Trades Advisory Councils monitored such accusations and sought to modify Jewish activities, while Jews in particular areas which were regarded as being unusually 'sensitive' such as Swiss Cottage or Golders Green were given advice on how to modify their 'obtrusive' behaviour.

The basic problem was that of reaction to provocation, particularly with regard to demonstrations in the East End itself. Here the two organisations had fundamentally different opinions. The Board urged Jews to stay away, while the JPC urged equally strongly that Fascist provocation should be met by counter-actions by the local Jews.

There was no way in which these two approaches could be combined without the application of a great deal of external pressure, and that eventually came from two sources –

Governmental intervention to prevent uniformed provocative marches and understanding of the real threat presented by Hitler's policies in Germany. The two organisations, under these circumstances, tried to reach agreement, but the attempts foundered on the extent to which the JPC could continue as an independent organisation.

At issue was the basic question as to whether the Board was the recognised forum in which all the issues affecting British Jewry should be discussed and decided. The JPC could see only one issue as being important, whereas the Board was rightly concerned to examine not only the issue of 'Defence' but also wider issues affecting the entire community. These were just as important, and it is an exclusive concentration on the issue of 'anti-semitism' which has distorted analysis of the 1930s.

Some of these issues might seem in the light of the impending catastrophe to be very minor, but they loomed large for many in the community then, and indeed have continued to be a source of controversy. One of these concerned the relative position of the Board and its Ecclesiastical Authorities. It was only possible to secure approval by the Board of a 'marriage secretary' if the 'Ecclesiastical Authorities' had approved of the Congregation. As a result of the controversies of the middle and late nineteenth centuries there were congregations of the 'right' and 'left' which had not secured such recognition.

The West London Synagogue had not been able to secure such approval from the Board, and indeed it had eventually to secure a special Act of Parliament. Nor was it prepared to send Deputies to the Board until guarantees were given that this accession did not impose on it the necessity of following any rulings which might be given by the respective ecclesiastical authorities. Thereafter various Reform communities did agree to affiliate to the Board, but the issue of 'marriage secretaries' continued to bedevil communal politics; it was only as the result of the possibility of a balance between various Reform and ultra-orthodox congregations that some immediate compromise was achieved.

There were still to be congregations denied such registration until they in their turn secured it by Act of Parliament. The issue of the extent to which the Board was bound to obey the decisions of its ecclesiastical authorities as distinct from paying attention to such rulings remained unresolved.

The most obvious problem however, apart from the issue of anti-semitism, continued to be the relationship between the Board and the Zionist movement. There continued to be a strong anti-Zionist movement parallel to that in support of the Zionist movement, and certainly there was a strong lobby on the Board organised, amongst others, by Lavy Bakstansky. He had become a member of the Board in 1934 and was anxious to bring the Board over to the side of the Zionist Federation.

The Board was still anxious to maintain its own position, seeing itself as representative of all elements within the Community. Closely linked with this was the move to set up a world-wide organisation to speak on behalf of world-wide Jewry in international affairs just as the Zionist Organisation did in affairs relating to Palestine.

At a meeting in 1936 in Geneva the World Jewish Congress was set up; the Board refused to be represented at Geneva, and insisted that only the Board could speak on behalf of British Jews. Even when various groups in Britain – several of them represented at the Board – established a 'British Section', the Board did its best to ensure that Governmental organisations paid no attention to the WJC in matters relating to British Jewry.

In consequence the Zionists on the Board turned their attention to increasing their influence on it. An opportunity came soon after the outbreak of the Second World War.

The war produced problems for all communal organisations within British Jewry. Some of them, like the United Synagogue, delegated authority in everyday matters to a small inner executive, in effect 'closing down' democratic procedures for the immediate future. The President of the Board, Neville Laski, in company with some of the leading members of the community, proposed a similar action for the Board, but there was considerable opposition to the suggestion and the most that could be achieved was a 'stream-lined Executive Committee' able to deal with emergencies.

Although a newly-elected deputy, Professor Selig Brodetsky, a strong supporter of the Zionist group, was closely involved with this move there was no suggestion that it was entirely a Zionist move. A further development came with the decision by Neville Laski to resign as President. Despite some initial opposition Brodetsky was elected unopposed; a preliminary circular from the Zionist group urged a full attendance at the election meeting. 'We are no longer prepared to be governed by a clique from above who have little contact with the masses of Jewry.'

His election however was not to be regarded as a direct 'take-over' of the Board; Brodetsky himself declared: 'I consider it the primary function of anybody who directs the activities of the Board of Deputies to conduct its affairs with due regard to the views of all sections of the Board.' He was as firmly attached to the maintenance of the Board's authority as any one could be:

> The Board must be the recognised central institution in Anglo-Jewry. It must be independent, democratic, representative of every section of the community, and not subservient to any person or section inside the Board, or to any group or organisation outside the Board.

One of the consequences of that approach was some differences of opinion between Brodetsky and Bakstansky, particularly at the time of the triennial elections of the Board in 1943. The Zionist group were canvassed very strongly, and the Report of the Board for 1943 reported 'an extraordinary increase in the number of Deputies elected and the number of constituencies which obtained representation for the new session ... an increase of 148 Deputies and 47 constituencies as compared with the end of the previous session'.

At the first session of the Board which following the elections, the link with the AJA was dissolved and although the 'caucus' was unable to secure a 'clean slate' of the honorary officers it was able to capture the various committees of the Board. Thereafter the Board worked closely with the Zionist groups in the country, at the same time however insisting that it was the Board which was the only legitimate representative of the community.

Brodetsky for example declared: 'The World Jewish Congress ... can have no right to carry out acts in this country in any sphere which may be interpreted as being on behalf of Anglo-Jewry'. Even when the Congress recognised the Board as the representative body of British Jewry both bodies insisted on retaining their freedom of action.

The significance of the 'capture' of the Board by the Zionist group related to the inter-connections between the Board and the wider community. The Zionist Federation became very powerful on the Board, most particularly in relation to the everyday working of the Board and the relations between the Zionist and the 'Independent' group, a relationship described as a 'phenomenon as near to a party system as the procedure, functions and history of a purely voluntary body such as the Board allowed'.

Above all, the Board had without question aligned itself to the Zionist side in the controversies which were to emerge over the establishment of the State of Israel.

Lucien Wolf, Secretary, Joint Foreign Committee, 1915–1930

THE MODERN COMMUNITY

The end of the war and the emergence of a Labour Government, combined with the urgent need to find a response to the catastrophe suffered by the Jews of Europe, had a marked impact upon the Board of Deputies. During the war the Zionist movement had taken a positive line in favour of an independent Jewish State, and the Board had come out in favour of that.

On the other hand, despite the frequent statements by the Labour Party in opposition that it supported the Zionist claim for a strengthening of the Jewish National Home, when it came into government it declared itself unable to implement these assurances, and the result was an open conflict between the Board and the Government. For the first time the issue of 'dual loyalties' came seriously to the front for many members of the Board, and even after the State of Israel had been established and recognised officially by the British Government the potential conflict of interests remained.

It became more intense when the Presidency of the Board came to be associated with membership of the House of Commons; so long as that office was primarily involved with internal community politics – or conflicts – it was still possible for the community to present a reasonably common front to the outside world. But when it began to be taken for granted – or even regarded as desirable – that the Board should turn to an individual who was prominent in national life, anomalies were bound to arise. When, for example, the President was a Member of Parliament he would eventually find a situation arising where his party allegiances and his responsibilities as President would come into conflict.

It would then be difficult for him either to vote according to the dictates of the party whips or to defy them. The most obvious occasions arose when Britain was directly or indirectly involved in the troubles of the Middle East, though there were to be other occasions when such clashes of interest arose.

The years immediately after the war saw great difficulties in Palestine between the Mandatory Government and the Jewish Agency, and such events as the hanging of two British sergeants in Palestine and the anti-Jewish riots which occurred in Britain resulted in great tensions. There were equally significant strains when the three major Middle East wars again brought the British Government into the conflicts, either as a result of direct British intervention or over the issue of supplies of arms to one side or the other. In a way, what had happened was a return to a rather earlier concept that the interests of the community would be best served by electing a 'notable' to the head of the most important British Jewish organisation.

When that had been Sir Moses Montefiore there had been occasions when tensions had arisen between his concept of the office and the ambitions of other members of the community, even though he had had no direct personal ambitions in political life; under the circumstances of this newer manifestation it was almost inevitable that such problems would arise.

A further set of problems which came even more to the fore in these years related to the balance between the metropolis and the provinces. This had been a problem from the very beginning of the modern history of the Board. But so long as the effective leadership of the community remained in the hands of a comparatively small group, the so-called 'Cousinhood', the problem remained comparatively minor. On occasions it erupted and even had some short-lived effect – as in 1917 – but with a growing 'democratisation' of the Board and a desire to see greater control exercised over its actions by its constituent organisations it became of much greater importance to the Board. While on the one hand the Board expressed itself anxious to bring the communities outside London more actively into support of the Board, both financially and by way of recruitment of 'fresh blood', it became progressively more difficult to translate this into practice.

Even the practice of holding full meetings of the Board in

THE BOARD OF DEPUTIES OF BRITISH JEWS

Meeting of European Branch of World Jewish Congress, Brussels, 1980

one or other of the major provincial centres could not do much in the way of attracting such support, and inevitably as the Board became more 'bureaucratised' the central officers of the Board found themselves increasingly tied to London. In the past too, a great element of the strength of the Board, as with many others of the institutions of the community, had been the continuing recruitment of individual 'provincials'; but the mid-years of the century saw a gradual decline in the strength of the non-London communities, and that too presaged future problems not only for the Board but for the British Jewish community as a whole.

A solution was found to one of the problems left over from the Second World War. The 'rift' between the Board and the WJC was healed by the decision of the Board to affiliate with the Congress, thus removing the need for a British Section of the Congress. At the same time this created new opportunities for the Board, in that it thereby gained access to a European scene and was thus enabled to have some impact upon a

European arena at a time when Britain itself was gaining such access through the 'Common Market'.

But perhaps the most fundamental problem for the whole future of the Board arose out of a long-running clash within the Board over the extent to which it was bound to follow the guidance given by the 'Ecclesiastical Authorities' of the Board.

The issues were inevitably a confusion between political and religious conflicts, and what was at stake was not merely the nature of the community as a whole but the extent to which the Board was representative of all shades of opinion in the community. It had been foreshadowed in the conflicts of the middle of the nineteenth century, and had been given further substance in the disputes of the inter-war years; but it erupted violently again in the early 1970s, and has come up again on occasions thereafter.

Originally the Board had been the creation of various synagogues, and these had been prepared to write into the Constitution of the Board reference to the religious authorities of those bodies. The Ashkenazi congregations had had the position of the Chief Rabbi safeguarded, while the Sephardi had done the same for the Haham; Sir Moses Montefiore, who had had a foot in both camps, was prepared to support both.

The advent of the West London Synagogue had been disapproved by both, and the result was that it had been excluded from the Board for over forty years. When it returned to the Board it did so on the clear understanding that it was not bound by any ecclesiastical ruling given by the Board.

Similarly, when other Liberal and Reform congregations were admitted to membership of the Board they too were given similar undertakings. Nonetheless there was an obvious feeling of disquiet, since their status was never quite the same as that of those congregations which did recognise the authority of one or other of the existing ecclesiastical heads.

When the Board was invited to submit evidence to the Government or Parliament on such issues as Shechita, marriage laws, or religious education the most that these con-

THE BOARD OF DEPUTIES OF BRITISH JEWS

A Board Meeting, 1978, Lord Fisher presiding

Lord Shinwell's 100th Birthday, 1984

THE MODERN COMMUNITY

gregations could do was to secure 'consultative status', and the Board speaking nominally on behalf of the community as a whole was obviously speaking on behalf of the Orthodox element within it.

With the growth within these synagogues of a new organisation and even a new 'militancy', an element of dissatisfaction emerged, and this came to the fore with an attempt to revise the Constitution of the Board in such a way as to give official consultative status to the 'Ecclesiastical Authorities' of the Reform congregations.

The story of that controversy is not at an end, and the attempts in 1971 and in 1984 to secure agreed solutions to the problem cannot be regarded as definitive; in a sense it is a problem which goes to the very root of the Board, for it asks the question of the extent to which the Board is a purely secular body or is supposed to represent the attitudes of British Jewry in all of its various aspects.

There is little way in which the 'outside world' can understand these various problems, if only because that world expects the community to be able to talk with a united voice on all aspects of its life, almost as if it were parallel to the Continental view of a 'gemeinde' to which all Jews should belong. In many ways a 'secular' Board might seem attractive, but it would not fulfil all the needs of the community and it would be out of line with the ways in which the community and the Board had developed.

Throughout its history the Board has always insisted on its role as the only official intermediary between the British Jewish community and the State, whether that be the central government or any other of its myriad organisms. The archives of the Board illustrate particularly this aspect of its work; whether there were complaints of open anti-semitism or instances of racial or religious discrimination, the Board continued to make itself the spokesman of the whole community.

The mere titles of some of these files make this point clear; they show complaints about abuses of the Sunday Trading Acts, missionary activities, requests that special provision be

THE BOARD OF DEPUTIES OF BRITISH JEWS

Meeting with the Liberian Ambassador, 1983; Messrs. H. Diamond, M. Benjamin, M. Savitt, G. Janner

H.M. The Queen with the President of the Board, Ald. Michael Fidler, JP, at a reception to mark the Centenary of the United Synagogue, 1970

made for Jewish students who wish not to have to sit examinations on Sabbaths or Festivals, the provision of Kosher food for prisoners or internees, the rights of Jews who had not yet been naturalised but who were being discriminated against over housing, the defence of Shechita – no item was too small or insignificant for the Board to be involved on behalf of members of the community.

Nor was any complainant too minor a member of the community for the President himself to be involved in these activities. Over and over again the files between President and Secretary indicate the great care taken by the official heads of the Board in all of its detailed activities. The files are much fuller for the period of the 1920s onwards, partly as a result of the work of two secretaries, Messrs. Rich and Zaiman, who brought particular expertises to their work, but partly also as an indication of the ways in which the community was coming even more strikingly to turn to the Board for assistance.

As the community itself – or rather as the children of the immigration – took more confidence and began to assert their rights within the community so the Board took a more active part in their problems.

The files show also the growing importance of the Board in relation to the affairs of Jewish communities outside the country. Just as in the nineteenth century Sir Moses Montefiore had been the recipient of messages and calls for assistance from all over the world so in the twentieth century the Board itself assumed his mantle.

The Foreign Affairs Committee of the Board shows contacts of very many different sorts; individual pleas for assistance are mingled with desperate appeals from communities as a whole, and the whole despairing history of Eastern Europe throughout the years following the First World War could be written almost completely from the Board's papers. The war itself saw no let-up in the flow of correspondence, and again the Holocaust too is reflected in the Board.

Links with the Empire and Commonwealth show the part played not merely by the Board but by the British Jewish

THE BOARD OF DEPUTIES OF BRITISH JEWS

Mr. James Callaghan, MP, the Prime Minister, with Lord Fisher of Camden, President of the Board of Deputies, 1977

Officers of the Board at No. 10 Downing Street, November 1985; l. to r. Hon. Treasurer Jeffrey Pinnick, Secretary-General Hayim Pinner, President Dr. Lionel Kopelowitz, the Prime Minister, Mrs. Margaret Thatcher; Vice-Presidents Eric Moonman and Victor Lucas.

community, and if imitation is the sincerest form of flattery the creation of parallel bodies, for example in South Africa, reflects the appreciation from outside the community of Great Britain of the part played by the Board.

At the same time the links between Government and Board were not merely one way. It was of importance for the Government to have a recognised body to approach in order to discover whether there was such a thing as a recognised Jewish point of view. Whether it was in relation to the Aliens Immigration Commission of the early part of the century, or changes in the law relating to Divorce or Family Law in the later part, it was to the Board that the Government would turn, and it is that facet of the work which makes the arguments over the 'Ecclesiastical Authorities' of the Board, and the part to be played by the 'Ecclesiastical Authorities' of those constituent bodies which do not recognise either the Chief Rabbi or the Haham, so very important for the Board and for the community as a whole.

In the meantime all the routine work of the Board does and must continue. Its various committees have to keep a watchful eye open for what might concern the community. Shechita must be protected, marriage secretaries must be registered, disused cemeteries must be kept in good order, anti-semitism must be combatted – all of the myriad needs of the community must be served and the Officers of the Board, elected and permanent alike, are kept busy, for the needs of British Jewry are endless.

The strength of the Board has always been its ability to recognise the development of new needs and its ability to set 'new needs' into the context of existing problems. Little has been said about the unceasing 'daily grind' of the Board, the work which takes up no headlines. Much of it impinges very strongly however upon the whole issue of the future of the community. Even such a unit as the Statistical Unit of the Board presents issues of the greatest possible significance to the Board and the community. Such simple questions as the size of the present-day community and the extent of its syna-

THE BOARD OF DEPUTIES OF BRITISH JEWS

Sir Barnett Janner with President Ben-Zvi in Jerusalem in 1960

President Shazar with a Board delegation in Jerusalem in 1970

gogal attendance can become highly debatable issues in the context of the community as a whole. There is nothing done by the Board which is so insignificant as to allow it to be dismissed as irrelevant.

At the same time there is inevitably a question-mark over the Board, arising out of its very success in making itself more 'democratic'. It has transformed itself into a body no longer dependent on the support of a small inner group but having to turn to a wider public; it has not managed to secure the support of that public in terms of adequate financial resoures or in terms of wholehearted realisation by the public of the need to maintain it in being as an organisation.

As an institution it can look back on a long fruitful history. Whether its origins are taken from the meetings of December 1760 or of March 1835 it has over the years played a vital role in the growth and development of British Jewry. If it is to continue to do so then it, in company with British Jewry itself, must look once again very carefully at what it is trying to do.

THE BOARD OF DEPUTIES OF BRITISH JEWS

Mr. Menachem Begin, Prime Minister of Israel, addressing the Board in 1979

H. E. Yehuda Avner, Ambassador of Israel, speaking to the Board, 1983

THE MODERN COMMUNITY

H.E. Chaim Herzog, President of Israel, at the Board of Deputies.

THE BOARD OF DEPUTIES OF BRITISH JEWS

November 1982 – courtesy call at No. 10 by leaders of the newly-formed Commonwealth Jewish Council

The Board in action – the President takes a question from a Deputy at a provincial meeting.

THE MODERN COMMUNITY

The Board promotes books of Jewish interest.

THE BOARD OF DEPUTIES OF BRITISH JEWS

A commemoration meeting to mark Yom Ha'Shoah (Holocaust Day) at the Savoy Theatre, 1984

Laying a weath at Auschwitz on the 40th Anniversary of the Warsaw Ghetto Uprising, 1983

THE MODERN COMMUNITY

October 1970: Soviet Jewry demonstration during London visit of Russian Foreign Minister Gromyko.

No to the PLO! mass rally in Trafalgar Square, July 1981, organised by the Board.

THE BOARD OF DEPUTIES OF BRITISH JEWS

Sir Sigmund Sternberg, JP, Martin Savit and Hayim Pinner with Dr. C. Schoneveld, General Secretary ICCJ, October 1980.

Central Enquiry Desk and Communal Diary: Mr Harold Altman, Director, with some of the volunteers celebrating the CED's 2nd anniversary, February 1984.

THE MODERN COMMUNITY

Charles H. L. Emanuel, Solicitor and Secretary of the Board, 1894–1926: Hon. Solicitor, 1926–1960

Sampson Samuel, Secretary and Solicitor, 1837–1869

THE BOARD OF DEPUTIES OF BRITISH JEWS
PAST PRESIDENTS OF THE BOARD

1760	Benjamin Mendes da Costa
1766	Joseph Salvador
1778	Joseph Salvador
1789	Moses Isaac Levy
1801	Naphtaly Bazevy
1802–1812	(No record)
1812	Raphael Brendon
1817–1829	Moses Lindo
1829–1835	Moses Moncatta
1835–1838	Moses Montefiore
1838–1840	David Salomons (later Sir David Salomons)
1838–1840	I. Q. Henriques
1840 (May–July)	Sir Moses Montefiore
1840–1841	Hananel de Castro (pro tem.)
1841–1846	Sir Moses Montefiore
1846 (March–August)	David Salomons
1846–1855	Sir Moses Montefiore
1855 (April–December)	Isaac Foligno
1855–1857	Sir Moses Montefiore
1857 (February–September)	Isaac Foligno
1857–1862	Sir Moses Montefiore
1862–1868	Joseph Mayer Montefiore (pro tem.)
1868 (June–November)	Sir Moses Montefiore
1868–1871	Joseph Mayer Montefiore (pro tem.)
1871–1874	Sir Moses Montefiore
1874–1880	Joseph Mayer Montefiore
1880–1895	Arthur Cohen, Q.C., M.P.
1895–1903	Sir Joseph Sebag-Montefiore
1903–1917	David Lindo Alexander, K.C.
1917–1922	Sir Stuart H. Samuel, Bt.
1922–1925 (November)	Henry S. Q. Henriques, K.C.
1925–1926 (January)	Lord Rothschild (acting)
1926–1933	O. E. d'Avigdor-Goldsmid, D.L., J.P. (later Sir Osmond E. d'Avigdor-Goldsmid, Bt.)
1933–1939	Neville J. Laski, Q.C. (later Judge Laski)
1940–1949	Professor Selig Brodetsky
1949–1955	Dr. A. Cohen
1955–1964	Sir Barnett Janner, M.P. (later Lord Janner)
1964 (June)	Ald. Michael M. Fidler, J.P.
1964–1967	S. Teff
1967–1973	Ald. Michael M. Fidler, J.P.
1973–1979	Ald. Sir Samuel (later Lord) Fisher
1979–1985	Hon. Greville Janner, Q.C., M.P.
1985–	Dr. Lionel Kopelowitz, J.P.

THE LAST HALF CENTURY

There were nine Presidents of the Board between 1933 and 1985.

NEVILLE LASKI KC   1933–39
His Presidency coincided with the rise of Hitler and the vicious anti-Jewish laws of the Nazi regime. At home, the anti-semitic manifestations of Mosley's Blackshirt movement led to the creation, during Laski's term of office, of the Jewish Defence Committee.

REV. ABRAHAM COHEN   1949–55
Abraham Cohen had had a distinguished career as a Hebrew and Talmudic scholar, and as Minister of the Birmingham Hebrew Congregation, when invited to take office as President of the Board.

PROFESSOR SELIG BRODETSKY 1939–49
The first East European Jew and the only academic to have held the post of President, Brodetsky's election marked the beginning of the 'Zionist' character of the Board. He steered the community during the difficult days of the Second World War and its immediate aftermath. Among the innumerable tasks he faced were the evacuation problems, the Blitz, the appalling revelation of the Nazi death camps, the post-war refugee problems, the struggle against the Mandate, culminating in the miraculous birth of the State of Israel.

THE BOARD OF DEPUTIES OF BRITISH JEWS

BARNETT JANNER MP
1955–64 (later LORD JANNER)

Barnett Janner was the first President of the Board since the late nineteenth century to sit as a Member of Parliament. Simultaneously occupying the position of President of the Zionist Federation, he rigorously championed Israel's cause in Parliament.

ABRAHAM MOSS   1964

After a distinguished career in local Government in Manchester, 'Abs' Moss was elected to the Presidency in June 1964, but tragically died less than a week later.

SOLOMON TEFF   1964–67

Solomon Teff, a Solicitor, had served as Chairman of the Erets Israel Committee for many years and was a natural choice for President after Moss's death.

THE LAST HALF CENTURY

MICHAEL FIDLER MP 1967–73
Michael Fidler had also been prominent in local Government in the Manchester area, and was subsequently elected to Parliament in 1970. He had the tremendous task of ensuring the solid support of the Community for Israel in the period immediately after the Six Day War. He laid the foundation for the Board's joining the World Jewish Congress.

SIR SAMUEL FISHER 1973–79
(later LORD FISHER OF CAMDEN)
A great local Government personality in London, he was Mayor of both Stoke Newington and Camden. 'Sammy' Fisher was unanimously elected President in June 1973, and in spite of poor health during the subsequent six years, ensured that the esteem of the Board grew even more. Once the Board became a participant in WJC, he held distinguished office in that organisation as chairman of the Governing Board, and undertook many overseas tours.

THE HON. GREVILLE JANNER, QC, MP 1979–85
Greville Janner, the immediate Past President and the son of Lord Janner, was elected to Parliament in 1970. Among his achievements in an eventful period of office were the establishment of the Commonwealth Jewish Council and the dedication of the Holocaust Memorial in Hyde Park.

THE BOARD OF DEPUTIES OF BRITISH JEWS

There were three Chief Executives of the Board between 1934 and 1985.

ABRAHAM MARKS   1964–67

ADOLPH BROTMAN   1934–66

HAYIM PINNER   1977–